感恩节

Customs, Traditions and Landmarks |
Non-Fiction Series

Copyright © 2022 by Level Learning, INC. and Washington Yu Ying PCS™
Original and Edited Text Copyright © 2022 by Washington Yu Ying PCS™

All rights reserved. No part of this book in whole or part may be reproduced without written permission from the publisher.

Published by Level Learning, INC.
Content Contributors:
Washington Yu Ying PCS™
Level Learning - Jingyao Qi

Illustrations by: Josh Taira

Leveling classification based on Level Learning standard. For full description, visit www.levellearning.com

ISBN 978-1-64040-014-6
Simplified Chinese Edition

About Level Learning:
Level Learning provides a literacy focused curriculum specifically designed for K-12 Chinese as a Second Language classrooms. Our program offers 20 levels of specific and detailed objectives, leveled texts and passages, mastery-based online assessment, and analytics to enable data-driven instruction. Level Learning reading curriculum for both literature and informational text emphasize grammar and comprehension skills to help teachers develop confident and independent Chinese language readers. The non-fiction series of books are specifically designed to support our informational text course based on multiple national standards. To learn more about our entire offering, visit www.levellearning.com.

About Washington Yu Ying PCS™:
Washington Yu Ying PCS is a Mandarin English dual language immersion International Baccalaureate (IB) World school. Yu Ying's mission is to inspire and prepare young people to create a better world by challenging them to reach their full potential in a nurturing Chinese/English educational environment. Yu Ying's comprehensive IB, dual immersion curriculum equips students with global competencies for success in the real world. As a leader in immersion education, Yu Ying is determined to advance Chinese language programs and global citizenry education by helping other schools create and strengthen their Chinese programs. For more information, email: products@washingtonyuying.org

十一月

星期一	星期二	星期三	星期四	星期五	星期六	星期日
	1	2	3	4	5	6
7	8	9	10	11	12	13
14	15	16	17	18	19	20
21	22	23	(24)	25	26	27
28	29	30				

感恩节是美国的传统节日。每年十一月的第四个星期四是美国人庆祝感恩节的日子。

这个节日为什么被称为"感恩节"呢?感恩节有什么传统呢?

1620年，一些英国人坐船来到了美洲。他们的食物很快吃光了，也有很多人来到美洲后生病死了。

这时，生活在美洲的原住民帮助了这些英国人，他们教这些英国人捕鱼和种菜。

那一年的秋天，英国人和原住民的土地都大丰收了。

这些英国人感谢神让他们平安地到达了美洲,也感谢原住民让他们有了大丰收。

他们用火鸡和南瓜做成美食来感谢原住民的帮助，所以这一天被称为"感恩节"。直到现在，火鸡和南瓜派都是感恩节的传统食物。

现在的感恩节,人们会和家人一起庆祝,感恩美好的生活。

你们庆祝感恩节吗？怎么庆祝呢？

Glossary

	Pinyin	English Definition
感恩节	gǎn ēn jié	Thanksgiving
美国	měi guó	U.S.A.
传统	chuán tǒng	tradition
节日	jié rì	festival
庆祝	qìng zhù	to celebrate
英国	yīng guó	United Kingdom
美洲	měi zhōu	North America
食物	shí wù	food
生病	shēng bìng	sick
死	sǐ	to die
原住民	yuán zhù mín	natives
捕鱼	bǔ yú	to fish
种菜	zhòng cài	to grow crops
秋天	qiū tiān	autumn
丰收	fēng shōu	to harvest

	Pinyin	English Definition
感谢	gǎn xiè	thanks
神	shén	God
平安	píng ān	safely
到达	dào dá	to arrive
火鸡	huǒ jī	turkey
南瓜	nán guā	pumpkin
美好	měi hǎo	good, wonderful
生活	shēng huó	life

www.ingramcontent.com/pod-product-compliance
Lightning Source LLC
Chambersburg PA
CBHW041223070526
44584CB00001B/61